Guion

THE LION

A Mindful Activity Book

ALL ABOUT ME

MY BIRTHDAY

MY NAME

MY DREAM JOB

MY FAVORITE SONGS

MY FAVORITE COLOR

THINGS I LIKE TO WEAR

FOODS I LIKE TO EAT

MY BEST FRIENDS

MY HOBBIES

MY FAVORITE BOOKS

MY FAVORITE SUBJECTS

MY FAVORITE ANIMALS

MY LIKES AND DISLIKES

Color in the emoji that best describes how you feel about each activity.

RIDING A BIKE

LISTENING TO MUSIC

HOMEWORK

READING A BOOK

FAMILY VACATION

HANGING WITH FRIENDS

HOUSE CHORES

PLAYING VIDEO GAMES

BEING OUTDOORS

Free to Imagine

CREATIVITY

TAKES

COURAGE

-Henri Matisse

WHAT IS YOUR SECRET IDENTITY?

1 Combine the first letter of your first name,

A: CREATIVE
B: FABULOUS
C: DARING
D: WILD
E: ADVENTUROUS
F: KIND
G: INSPIRING
H: COURAGEOUS
I: TALENTED
J: EXTRAORDINARY
K: DAZZLING
L: AWESOME
M: WONDERFUL
N: TENACIOUS
O: PHENOMENAL
P: TERRIFIC
Q: WISE
R: BOLD
S: CURIOUS
T: FEARLESS
U: FUN
V: JOYFUL
W: PLAYFUL
X: SENSATIONAL
Y: HAPPY
Z: GRACEFUL

2 And the month of your birthday!

JANUARY: FRIEND
FEBRUARY: DREAMER
MARCH: SPIRIT
APRIL: BEING
MAY: SOUL
JUNE: LEADER
JULY: WARRIOR
AUGUST: CREATOR
SEPTEMBER: HEART
OCTOBER: GENIUS
NOVEMBER: HERO
DECEMBER: EXPLORER

My Secret Identity is:

____

____

MY FAMILY AND FRIENDS

Draw pictures of your loved ones.

THINK BELIEVE DREAM AND DARE

THIS OR THAT?

Check the best answers for you.
Compare answers with a friend.

☐	TRUTH	OR	DARE	☐
☐	CHOCOLATE	OR	CANDY	☐
☐	JUICE	OR	SODA	☐
☐	SINGING	OR	DANCING	☐
☐	COMEDIES	OR	DRAMAS	☐
☐	BURGER	OR	PIZZA	☐
☐	CATS	OR	DOGS	☐
☐	SWEET	OR	SALTY	☐
☐	SILVER	OR	GOLD	☐
☐	WIZARD	OR	NINJA	☐
☐	SNEAKERS	OR	SANDALS	☐
☐	POPCORN	OR	ICE CREAM	☐
☐	TATER TOTS	OR	FRENCH FRIES	☐
☐	LAPTOP	OR	TABLET	☐
☐	SUNNY	OR	RAINY	☐
☐	MOUNTAINS	OR	BEACH	☐
☐	BOARD GAMES	OR	VIDEO GAMES	☐

SELF-CONFIDENCE

Write down different reasons you are an awesome person!

I am awesome because

Curious

FEELINGS MATCHING

Draw a line from the emotion to the picture that you think is the best match.

CONFUSED

AMUSED

HAPPY

SAD

SATISFIED

EXCITED

PLEASED

PROUD

WORRIED

ANNOYED

EMOJI SUDOKU

Write in the letter for each missing picture.
Remember, an image must appear only once
in each row, column, and square grid.

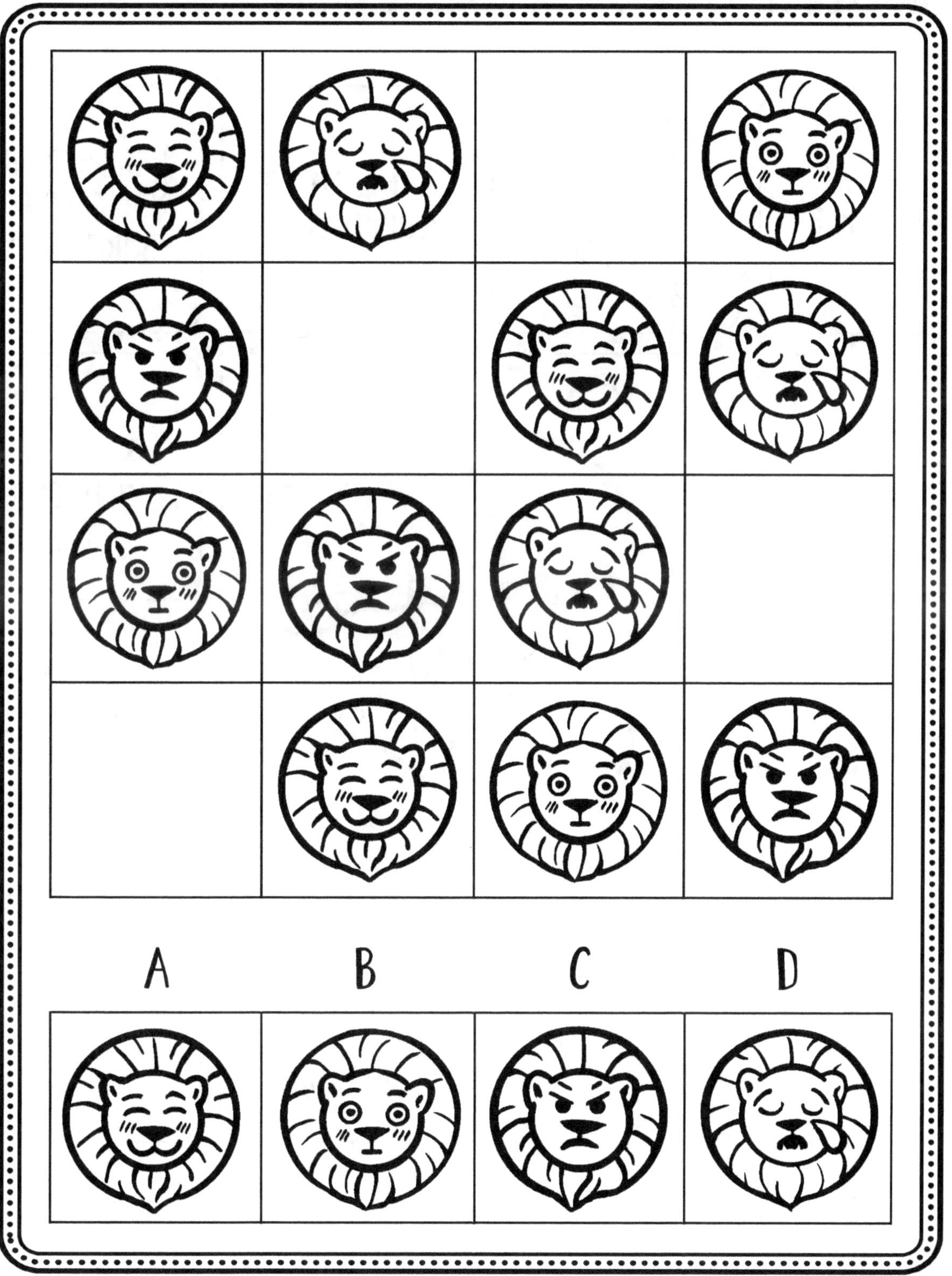

KINDNESS BINGO

Cross off each square as you explore different ways of being kind.

SMILE AT TEN PEOPLE.	STICK A NICE NOTE INTO SOMEONE'S DESK OR BACKPACK.	COMPLIMENT TWO PEOPLE.	MAKE A THANK YOU CARD FOR YOUR TEACHER.
HOLD THE DOOR OPEN FOR SOMEONE.			GIVE SOMEONE A HIGH FIVE.
SIT WITH A NEW PERSON OR GROUP AT LUNCH.			CLEAN SOMETHING WITHOUT BEING ASKED.
CREATE YOUR OWN KIND DEED.	ASK SOMEONE HOW THEIR DAY IS GOING.	LEARN TO SAY "THANK YOU" IN A NEW LANGUAGE.	TELL SOMEONE YOU LOVE THEM.

LET KINDNESS BE CONSTANT

ME AND MY FRIEND

Guion the Lion and Rae the Bushbaby are best friends.
They are different in many ways. For example,
Guion has a colorful imagination, while Rae is very practical.

THINK OF A GOOD FRIEND.
HOW ARE YOU AND YOUR FRIEND DIFFERENT?

HOW ARE YOU THE SAME?

BEING A FRIEND

Rae tried really hard to see what her friend Guion wanted her to see because she wanted to be a good friend.

WHAT DO YOU DO TO BE A GOOD FRIEND?

HOW DO YOU WANT
TO BE TREATED BY FRIENDS?

Friendship

DON'T GIVE UP!

**Sometimes friends see things differently.
Although Rae couldn't see what Guion wanted her to see,
he didn't give up and kept trying to show her new things.**

WHAT IS SOMETHING DIFFICULT YOU'VE DONE
EVEN THOUGH YOU WANTED TO QUIT AT TIMES?

WHY DID YOU KEEP TRYING?

DRAW A PICTURE OR WRITE ABOUT HOW YOU FEEL.

MINDFULNESS SCAVENGER HUNT

Try to find each of these things in your surroundings.

- [ ] SOMETHING THAT IS YOUR FAVORITE COLOR.
- [ ] AN OBJECT YOU CAN USE TO MAKE A GIFT.
- [ ] SOMETHING YOU HAVE NEVER SEEN BEFORE.
- [ ] A THING THAT MAKES YOU SMILE.
- [ ] A SIGN OR ITEM WITH A WORD YOU DON'T KNOW ON IT.
- [ ] SOMETHING THAT MAKES YOU THINK OF A FRIEND.
- [ ] AN INTERESTING PATTERN OR TEXTURE.
- [ ] A THING THAT MAKES A NOISE.
- [ ] SOMETHING THAT HAS A GOOD SMELL.
- [ ] A THING THAT IS USEFUL.

Mistakes

are

PROOF

that I am

TRYING

I CAN DO HARD THINGS
I AM BRAVE
LIFE IS TOUGH, BUT SO AM I
EVERY DAY IS AN ADVENTURE
I AM KIND
I AM ONE OF A KIND
I KEEP GOING
I HAVE BIG DREAMS

DESIGN BUTTONS

Use the positive affirmations on the left to design some cool buttons below.

You are Worth

GUION

Celebrating!

www.ingramcontent.com/pod-product-compliance
Lightning Source LLC
LaVergne TN
LVHW080208180826
845678LV00023BA/1981

* 9 7 9 8 3 5 0 7 0 2 5 1 4 *